GOD MADE DIRT

A Christian Kids' Book About Creation | By KL Piazza

Copyright © 2016 Kevin L Piazza. All rights reserved.

Scripture quotations from The Authorized (King James) Version, Public Domain.
Rights in the Authorized Version in the United Kingdom are vested in the Crown.
Reproduced by permission of the Crown's patentee, Cambridge University Press.

To my children,
and my children's children.

But the mercy of the Lord is from everlasting
to everlasting upon them that fear him,
and his righteousness unto children's children
Psalm 103:17

God made DIRT.

God made an ANT
that crawls on the dirt
that God made.

God made a BEE
that buzzes the ant
that crawls on the dirt
that God made.

God made a FLOWER
that feeds the bee
that buzzes the ant
that crawls on the dirt
that God made.

God made a CAT
that sniffs the flower
that feeds the bee
that buzzes the ant
that crawls on the dirt
that God made.

God made a DOG
that growls at the cat
that sniffs the flower
that feeds the bee
that buzzes the ant
that crawls on the dirt
that God made.

God made a HORSE
that neighs at the dog
that growls at the cat
that sniffs the flower
that feeds the bee
that buzzes the ant
that crawls on the dirt
that God made.

God made a TREE
that shades the horse
that neighs at the dog
that growls at the cat
that sniffs the flower
that feeds the bee
that buzzes the ant
that crawls on the dirt
that God made.

God made a RIVER
that waters the tree
that shades the horse
that neighs at the dog
that growls at the cat
that sniffs the flower
that feeds the bee
that buzzes the ant
that crawls on the dirt
that God made.

God made a MOUNTAIN
that holds the river
that waters the tree
that shades the horse
that neighs at the dog
that growls at the cat
that sniffs the flower
that feeds the bee
that buzzes the ant
that crawls on the dirt
that God made.

God made a CLOUD
that covers the mountain
that holds the river
that waters the tree
that shades the horse
that neighs at the dog
that growls at the cat
that sniffs the flower
that feeds the bee
that buzzes the ant
that crawls on the dirt
that God made.

God made the WIND
that blows the cloud
that covers the mountain
that holds the river
that waters the tree
that shades the horse
that neighs at the dog
that growls at the cat
that sniffs the flower
that feeds the bee
that buzzes the ant
that crawls on the dirt
that God made.

God made the SUN
that warms the wind
that blows the cloud
that covers the mountain
that holds the river
that waters the tree
that shades the horse
that neighs at the dog
that growls at the cat
that sniffs the flower
that feeds the bee
that buzzes the ant
that crawls on the dirt
that God made.

God made YOU
to play in the sun
that warms the wind
that blows the cloud
that covers the mountain
that holds the river
that waters the tree
that shades the horse
that neighs at the dog
that growls at the cat
that sniffs the flower
that feeds the bee
that buzzes the ant
that crawls on the dirt
that God made.

And the Lord God formed man of the dust of the ground, and
breathed into his nostrils the breath of life;
and man became a living soul.

Genesis 2:7

www.ingramcontent.com/pod-product-compliance
Lightning Source LLC
Chambersburg PA
CBHW041539040426
42446CB00002B/155